EVERYTHING SOCCER

NATIONAL GEOGRAPHIC KiDS

NATIONAL GEOGRAPHIC

WASHINGTON, D.C.

NATIONAL GEOGRAPHIC KiDS

EVERYTHING SOCCER

BY BLAKE HOENA
With Star Soccer Player OMAR GONZALEZ

CONTENTS

Throughout the world, soccer is a game played with or without specialized equipment, on grassy fields, on dirt yards, or even on the street. These boys are playing in Jinshang Park, a former royal garden that is now a park in Beijing, China.

Modern soccer stadiums can hold from 25,000 to 80,000 people in seats and standing sections. That's a lot of noisy, cheering fans!

INTRODUCTION

WHAT IS THE MOST
POPULAR SPORT IN THE WORLD?

No, not baseball. Not basketball either. And it isn't cricket, tennis, rugby, or hockey, even though those sports are played all over the globe and by millions of people. It's football! But don't confuse this football with American football, the game with quarterbacks who throw oval balls. We're talking *fútbol*, the sport you might know as soccer.

From huge coliseums that hold tens of thousands of people to small stadiums, local parks, and dusty streets, soccer is played everywhere and by *hundreds* of millions of people. It also has billions (yes billions with a *b*) of rowdy fans around the world cheering on their favorite teams. Why is it such a popular sport? Come see why this beautiful game scores big with so many people as you learn EVERYTHING there is to know about soccer.

EXPLORER'S CORNER

Hi! I'm Omar Gonzalez.
Professionally, I play for the L.A. Galaxy, but I'm also a member of the United States men's national soccer team. I started playing soccer when I was four years old. When my older siblings kicked the ball around, I would just jump into the mix. Plus, my uncle played professionally, so in a way, it's a family sport. My position is defender, like my uncle. But I played center midfielder and forward until college. My college coach put me at center back because he thought it was a more natural fit, and the rest is history. I was named the Major League Soccer (MLS) Defender of the Year in 2011.

Professional soccer players have excellent balance and concentration. Dribbling and using all parts of the foot to direct the ball are skills learned over time.

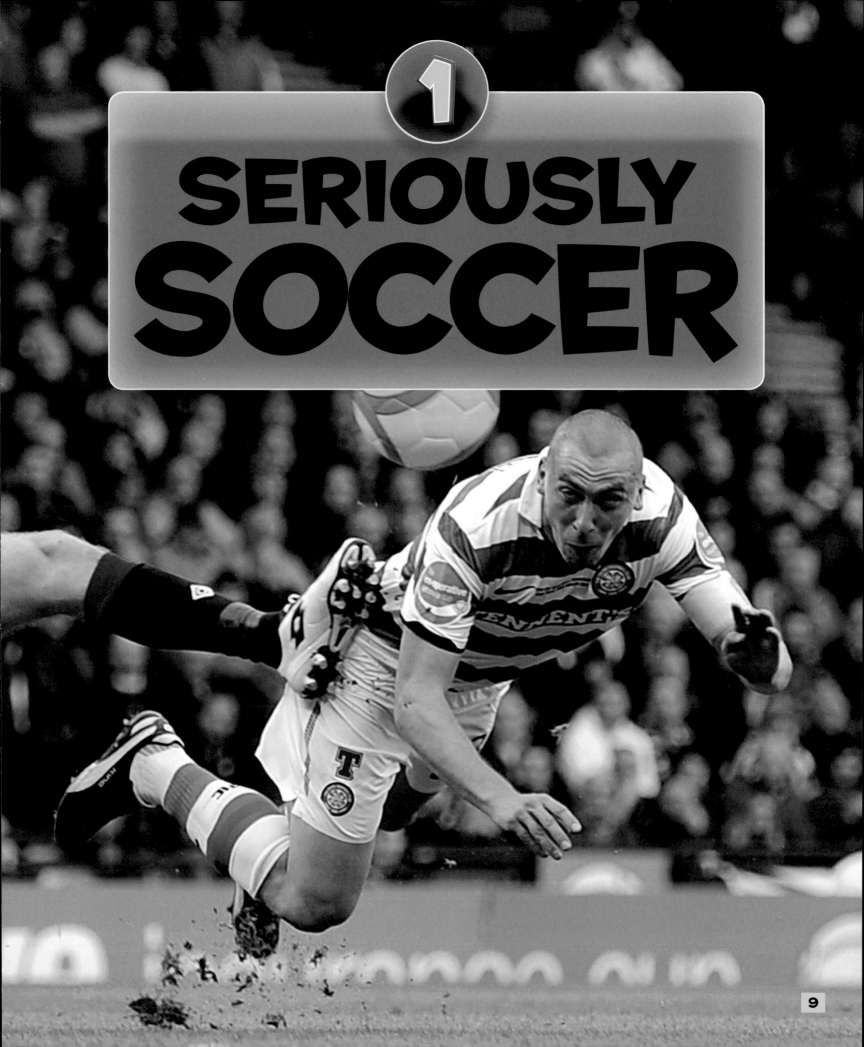

SERIOUSLY SOCCER

WHAT IS SOCCER?

SOCCER IS ONE OF THE

SIMPLEST GAMES TO PLAY. ALL YOU NEED

is a ball and an area to kick it around, whether that's a large soccer arena or your own backyard where a couple of trees serve as goalposts. Yet, a game of soccer can be as complicated as a chess match. Mastering the sport takes more than just quick feet and a powerful kick—it's a game of strategic smarts. Maybe that's why soccer is so popular. It can be a fun and easy game to play among friends; yet it can also be extremely challenging as professional teams pit their skills against each other.

SOCCER BASICS

TYPE OF PLAY: Team sport, with up to 11 players on a team

OBJECT OF THE GAME: Score more goals than your opponent.

FIELD OF PLAY: Just about any open space, from indoor stadiums to outdoor pitches, parks, backyards, and even the beach

KEY RULE TO THE GAME: Players cannot use their hands (except for the goalkeeper) while the ball is in play.

LAYING DOWN THE LAW

While kicking the ball around with friends, you probably only worry about the most basic rule of the game: getting the ball in the goal to score. The Fédération Internationale de Football Association (FIFA) is the organization that oversees how the game is played around the world. Formed in 1904, FIFA has a set of rules, called Laws of the Game, that leagues worldwide follow so that everyone is playing the same basic game. FIFA also holds the largest soccer tournament in the world, the World Cup.

KICKIN' IT A HEADER IS A GOAL SCORED FROM A HEAD BUTT TO THE BALL.

THE FIELD OF PLAY

A soccer field is called a pitch. The reason why is somewhat of a mystery, but it is thought to be based on the idea of staking poles into the ground, like you would to "pitch" a tent, to mark the playing area. The game of cricket was set up this way, and soccer players borrowed the term in the 1880s.

SOUND LIKE A SOCCER PRO

Understanding soccer lingo makes it easier to play or watch the game. Here are some common soccer terms:

BREAKAWAY—A sudden play in which one (or more) attacking players race downfield with the ball ahead of the defenders

DEFENDER—A player who is trying to prevent a goal from being scored

DRAW—Tie game or match

FOOTBALL CLUB (FC)—A soccer team

GOAL LINES—The sidelines of a soccer field

HEADER—Hitting the ball with your head

KIT—A player's equipment

MATCH—A soccer game

PITCH—A soccer field

STRIKER—A player who is trying to score a goal

TOUCHLINES—The lines on either side of the play area

SUPER SOCCER AWARDS

DON'T LET SOCCER'S LOW-SCORING GAMES FOOL YOU. THE ACTION MAY SEEM SLOW AT TIMES, BUT

there is a lot of strategizing going on during a game. Both teams try to find weaknesses in each other's defense. With one quick "killer pass," a player may break away for a goal. The crowd then rocks the stadium with their cheers. The action is quick and sudden, and it can be amazing. Here are some incredible soccer feats that will wow you.

YOUNGEST PLAYER TO SCORE A WORLD CUP GOAL

Edson Arantes do Nascimento, better known as Pelé, was 17 when he scored his first World Cup goal for Brazil. He is the only player ever to be a part of three World Cup winning teams.

Pelé, shown here near the end of his career, played from age 15 to 37.

MARTA

MOST WORLD CUP GOALS

When you are a soccer star in Brazil, you don't even need a last name! At least that's true for Ronaldo and Marta. Ronaldo Luís Nazário de Lima, known simply as Ronaldo, became the highest goal scorer in World Cup history in 2006, when he scored his 15th goal. Fellow Brazilian Marta Vieira da Silva, who wears a jersey with just her first name on the back, has scored 14 Women's World Cup goals—a joint record with German star Birgit Prinz.

LARGEST STADIUM

Estadio Azteca is the largest stadium dedicated to soccer. Located in Mexico City, Mexico, it gets deafening with more than 100,000 noisy fans rooting for the home team, Club América.

WILDEST KICK

The bicycle kick is one of the most difficult soccer kicks. It requires a player to have their back to the goal while throwing their legs up in the air, kicking the ball and falling backward. Sometimes called a scissor kick or overhead kick, it's a skill that only a few pros use to surprise the goalkeeper.

LONGEST HEADER GOAL

Ryujiro Ueda of the Fagiano Okayama FC in Japan must have a head as solid as a brick. He knocked a header a whopping 64 yards (58.6 m) to score a goal against rival team Yokohama FC in 2011.

OLDEST SOCCER CLUB

Sheffield FC, based out of South Yorkshire, England, has been knocking in goals since way back to 1857, before there were even official laws of the game.

KICKIN' IT BRAZIL'S MEN'S TEAM HAS BEEN IN THE WORLD CUP 20 TIMES.

A LONG HISTORY

WHERE DO YOU THINK SOCCER ORIGINATED? ENGLAND? NO. BRAZIL? NOPE. ITALY?

Nuh-uh. None of today's powerhouses of international soccer can lay claim to being the birthplace of the sport. *Cuju*, a game meaning "kick the ball with foot," was played more than 2,000 years ago in China and is considered an early version of soccer. Soccer-type games were played by groups and clubs all over the world, but standard rules for the game didn't exist until 1863, when 11 football clubs in England met to form the Football Association.

ASSOCIATION FOOTBALL

Bet you didn't know that soccer has an official name. Association football is the name of the modern game standardized by the Football Association. The rules the Association set made it easier for clubs from different areas to play matches. Before the Football Association, clubs had to set the rules of the game each time they played, and this caused arguments. Association football and its rules spread throughout the world.

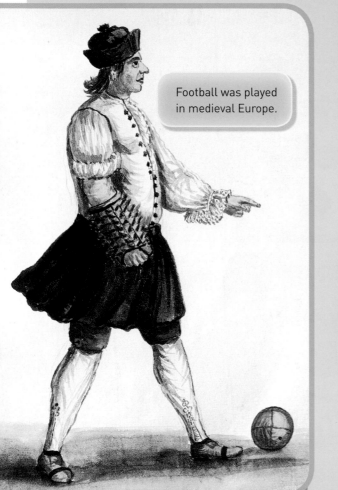

Football was played in medieval Europe.

Sunderland AFC was founded in 1879. AFC stands for Association Football Club.

SUNDERLAND A.F.C.
STADIUM OF LIGHT

SCOTLAND AND **ENGLAND** PLAYED THE **FIRST OFFICIAL** INTERNATIONAL SOCCER MATCH, IN **1872.** THE GAME ENDED IN A **TIE.**

KICKIN' IT EARLY SOCCER BALLS WERE MADE OUT OF INFLATED PIGS' BLADDERS.

HIP ME WITH YOUR BEST SHOT!

Ulama, an ancient Mesoamerican game, was played by two opposing teams knocking the ball back and forth with their hips. It's believed to be the first sport played with a rubber ball.

Ancient soccer balls were made from skulls or animal bladders. Even today, where soccer balls are too expensive, people make do with net-wrapped rubber balls.

ANCIENT GAME

More than 4,000 years ago, Greeks played a game called *episkyros*. Teams kicked and tossed the ball, trying to score by knocking the ball over their opponents' end line.

FOOTBALL VS. SOCCER

Why the two names? Well, the sport originally earned the name football, because players kicked the ball around with their feet. Seems simple enough. In the United States and Canada, football was a game based on rugby football, played with a ball that was more egg-shaped. To avoid confusion, football is called soccer in those two countries.

By the Numbers

14 players made up a episkyros team.

12 players was the maximum on a ulama team.

11 players per team are allowed on the field at one time in modern soccer.

Manchester United honored three of its most beloved players, George Best, Denis Law, and Sir Bobby Charlton, in a statue that sits in front of the club's stadium in Manchester, England.

A GLOBAL GAME

AS OF 2013, FIFA HAD 209 MEMBER ORGANIZATIONS

around the world. Soccer leagues exist on all continents (except Antarctica). Many countries also have professional leagues in which local teams play each other. There are also hundreds of thousands of amateur leagues, school teams, and youth associations. Not everyone can be a soccer star, but nearly 300 million soccer players throughout the world are out there playing their favorite sport—making soccer truly a global game.

UNITED STATES

While the United States men's team has never finished better than third in the World Cup, the women's team has never finished worse than third. The women won in 1991 and 1999. They have also racked up four Olympic gold medals and one silver.

NORTH AMERICA

UNITED STATES

2012 U.S. WOMEN'S OLYMPIC SOCCER TEAM

SOUTH AMERICA

URUGUAY

EXPLORER'S CORNER

Soccer is the world's sport because all you really need is a ball. This makes it affordable to play and easy to throw together a game with friends. And anything can be used for the goal: two shoes, garbage cans, a couple of trees. Soccer is also attractive to kids because it's a team sport with a lot of opportunities to play, from pickup games to amateur leagues. That's helping its popularity grow in the U.S. and around the world.

URUGUAY

Not only did Uruguay host the first World Cup in 1930, but its men's national team also won that championship. Estadio Centenario was built specifically for the first World Cup, and Uruguay paid the travel costs of the 13 teams that competed. Uruguay's national team won again in 1950 and came close with a fourth-place finish in 2010.

WORLD CUP WINNERS

MEN		WOMEN
Brazil 5	Uruguay 2	Germany 2
Italy 4	France 1	United States 2
Germany 3	England 1	Norway 1
Argentina 2	Spain 1	Japan 1

FIFA WORLD CUP

ENGLAND

Wembley Stadium is one of the world's most famous soccer stadiums and the scene of soccer championships, the 1948 Olympic Games, and many rock concerts. Soccer star Pelé called Wembley the "capital of football." The original stadium was built in 1923 and demolished in 2003. The new Wembley, opened in 2007, holds 90,000 people and is England's national stadium.

UNITED KINGDOM

SPAIN

E U R O P E

A S I A

JAPAN

SPAIN

Spain's Real Madrid is the world's richest football club. The club makes enough money to sign some of the world's top players. England's David Beckham, France's Zinedine Zidane, and Brazil's Robinho and Ronaldo have all played for Real Madrid. Real Madrid signed star player Cristiano Ronaldo to the sport's richest contract— $206 million for five years, in 2013.

A F R I C A

JAPAN

The World Cup was held for the first time in Asia in 2002. Teams played in stadiums across South Korea and Japan. Since then, Japan's national teams have taken off. Their men's team lost the bronze medal match to Korea in the 2012 Summer Olympics. The women's team was masterful in defeating the United States for the World Cup in 2011, and won a silver medal in the 2012 Summer Olympics.

VUVUZELA

SOUTH AFRICA

A U S T R A L I A

SOUTH AFRICA

No African country has won the World Cup. None have even made it to the semifinals. Yet in 2010, South Africa became the first African country to host the World Cup, at stadiums in Johannesburg, Cape Town, and Durban. South Africa's national men's team has appeared in three World Cups.

CRISTIANO RONALDO

ANTARCTICA

KICKIN' IT TINY URUGUAY, WITH ONLY 3.3 MILLION PEOPLE, HAS WON THE WORLD CUP TWICE.

A PHOTOGRAPHIC DIAGRAM

THE PITCH

SOCCER PITCHES

MAY SEEM GIGANTIC (THEY'RE bigger than American football fields), but don't worry about getting lost while kicking the ball around. Their size can vary depending on how much room is available and the age of the players competing against each other. For youth leagues, which often have teams of fewer than 11 players, the pitch can be half as big as what's described here. These dimensions are for adult, international matches regulated by FIFA.

IT'S EASY BEING GREEN

FIFA soccer rules specify the dimensions of a soccer pitch. Fields can be grass or artificial turf, but the playing surface must be green.

LENGTH	WIDTH
Min. 98 yards (90 m)	Min. 49 yards (45 m)
Max. 131 yards (120 m)	Max. 98 yards (90 m)

CORNER FLAGS

At the corners of the pitch, the flags help referees and players see where the touchlines and goal lines are.

CORNER ARC

1 yard (1 m) radius

The place where attacking teams take corner kicks.

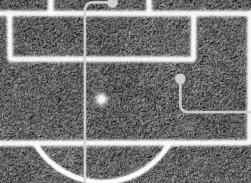

GOAL LINE

Lines along the width, and where the goals are, mark the edge of the playing field.

GOAL AREA

This area is 6 yards (5.5 m) deep, and 20 yards (18.3 m) long, and is where defending teams take goal kicks.

GOAL

The goal measures 8 yards (7.3 m) from post to post, and is 8 feet (2.4 m) high. It is where the goalkeeper defends the net.

TOUCHLINES

These lines along the length of the field mark the sides of the playing field.

MIDFIELD LINE

The midfield line divides the playing field in half.

CENTER CIRCLE

This circle, which is 10 yards (9 m) in radius, is where the kickoff takes place to start the game, and to restart the game after goals and halftime.

PENALTY ARC

Along with the penalty area, this is part of the pitch where defenders cannot enter during a penalty kick.

PENALTY AREA

At 18 yards (16.5 m) deep, and 44 yards (40 m) long, the penalty area is where penalty kicks are taken.

PENALTY SPOT

The ball is placed on the penalty spot when an attacking team takes a penalty kick. It is located 12 yards (11 m) from the goal.

Soccer is a game of angles and curves. The black hexagons on a soccer ball help players see the curves the ball makes when it is in play.

2
GET IN THE GAME

IT'S THE LAW!

EVERY SPORT HAS
RULES THAT GOVERN PLAY.

Soccer is no exception. The rules of soccer are called the Laws of the Game. Seventeen laws were made by FIFA, and they cover official league play. If you're playing in the backyard with your friends, you only need to worry about the basics. You can argue with each other about what is "fair." But if you want to have a greater understanding of the game while watching a professional match or the World Cup, here is a quick breakdown of the laws.

KICKIN' IT THE OFFICIAL LANGUAGES OF FIFA ARE ENGLISH, FRENCH, GERMAN, AND SPANISH.

LAYING DOWN THE LAW

Each year, FIFA produces a Laws of the Game guide. When teams squabble over whether a goal was a goal or how to substitute a player, the laws can be used to settle the dispute.

LAW 1
THE SIZE OF THE FIELD

Matches can be played on natural or artificial surfaces, but they must be green. The field must be rectangular and marked with lines to guide play.

LAW 2
THE BALL

The soccer ball must not be more than 28 inches (71 cm) and not less than 27 inches (68 cm) in circumference. The ball must be made of leather or another approved material.

LAW 3
THE NUMBER OF PLAYERS

Each team has at most 11 players, one of whom is the goalkeeper, with a minimum of 7 players for international play. This law also covers substitutions of players from the bench for those on the field.

LAW 4
THE PLAYERS' EQUIPMENT

Basic equipment includes jerseys, shorts, stockings (socks), shin guards, and footwear.

LAW 5
THE REFEREE

One referee controls the game. The laws outline the power and duties of the ref, including acting as a timekeeper and punisher of offenses.

LAW 6
THE ASSISTANT REFEREES

Two assistant referees help the referee make calls.

LAW 7
THE DURATION OF THE MATCH

A game consists of two equal halves, up to 45 minutes long.

LAW 8
THE START AND RESTART OF PLAY

A kickoff starts the game and restarts the game after each goal and begins the second half of the game. Often, a coin toss decides who kicks off to start the game.

LAW 9
THE BALL IN AND OUT OF PLAY

A ball is out of play when it completely crosses the goal line or touchline.

LAW 10
THE METHOD OF SCORING

A goal is scored when a ball completely crosses the goal line, between the goalposts.

LAW 11
OFFSIDE

Offside rules are probably the most confusing thing for soccer newbies to understand. The purpose of this law is to keep players from camping out next to the opposing goal in hopes of receiving a long pass and scoring an easy goal.

LAW 12
FOULS AND MISCONDUCTS

Fouls and misconducts are penalized with direct free kicks, penalty kicks, indirect free kicks, cautions, and sending off the field. Offenses include kicking, tripping, tackling, holding, spitting, touching the ball, and entering the field without permission.

LAW 13
FREE KICKS

There are two types of free kicks: direct and indirect. The laws outline when they are awarded (for fouls), who can take them (which players), and how a referee indicates a kick (with arm and hand signals).

LAW 14
PENALTY KICKS

There are ten possible offenses for which a penalty kick is awarded. The laws state the offenses, as well as where the ball must be placed and where the defending goalkeeper and other players can be located on the field.

LAW 15
THE THROW-IN

A throw-in occurs when a ball crosses one of the two touchlines. The thrower must face the field and throw the ball with both hands from behind and over his or her head.

LAW 16
THE GOAL KICK

When the attacking team kicks the ball across their opponent's goal line (and doesn't score a goal), the defending team gets a goal kick.

LAW 17
THE CORNER KICK

When a defending team knocks the ball across their own goal line, the attacking team gets a corner kick. These are dangerous for the defending team, as the player taking the corner kick tries to curve the ball in front of the goal for scoring opportunities.

PLACES, EVERYONE!

BASEBALL HAS PITCHERS
AND OUTFIELDERS, AND AMERICAN FOOTBALL has quarterbacks and linebackers. Soccer also has several different positions. While all players need to have solid footwork and passing abilities, each position has a required set of skills for a player to be successful. Here are the basics.

GLOVES AND GUTS

Goalkeepers are the only players allowed to use their hands, which is why they wear gloves. But that doesn't make their job any easier. They need to have guts to jump into the fray and sweep a ball from in front of the net. They must also be agile, diving to make saves on fast-moving balls, which is why those gloves are heavily padded.

TO THE RESCUE

Defenders (also called fullbacks) are the basis for any winning team. They are the muscle that helps protect a goalie. Having the strength and bravery to block attacking players is key for defenders to keep the opposing team from getting good shots on the goal. Defenders also need to excel at tackling, or intercepting the ball. Sometimes, a defender called a sweeper stays by the goal to provide an extra line of defense.

KICKIN' IT WINGERS ARE OFFENSIVE PLAYERS WHO STAY NEAR THE TOUCHLINES.

ON THE ATTACK!

Forwards are the speediest players on the pitch. Their main job is to take passes from midfielders and go on the attack, scoring goals. They must be quick and dead set on their goal. The opposing defenders will be out to stop them, so great dribbling skills are also a must. The center forward is called a striker, and this player is usually a team's top scorer.

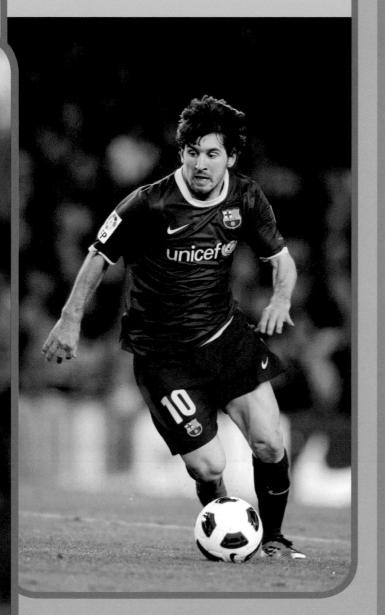

WE CAN DO IT ALL

Midfielders are the everything type of players. Covering the middle of the pitch, they must have a clear view of the game, knowing when to fall back on defense and when to go on the attack. They need to have great endurance, as they run around more than anyone else, and they must also be accurate passers to connect with a forward racing downfield on a breakaway.

4 DEFENDERS
4 MIDFIELDERS
2 FORWARDS

Once the most common, the 4-4-2 is a defensive-minded formation, with four midfielders working to stop an opposing team's forwards from mounting an attack.

4 DEFENDERS
2 MIDFIELDERS
4 FORWARDS

When late in the game and behind in the score, this formation is a strong offensive one, with a team's best goal scorers leading the attack.

3 DEFENDERS
4 MIDFIELDERS
3 FORWARDS

Putting equal importance on defense and offense, this balanced formation needs a great group of midfielders who can creep back to defend or rush forward to attack.

RED CARD!

EARLY ON IN SOCCER'S HISTORY,
THERE WEREN'T ANY REFEREES. SOCCER WAS
considered a game played between gentlemen, who would never purposely foul or try to take advantage of each other. As the sport grew more competitive, too many arguments broke out, often delaying games as teams fought over those calls. Referees have been on-field rule enforcers since the late 1800s. They oversee the game and hand out punishments to players and teams that don't play according to the rules.

YOU'RE OFF!
For the most serious offenses, such as purposely hurting another player or spitting, a referee will show a player a red card. That player is "sent off," or must leave the game. The player is usually suspended for the following game, or sometimes more, depending on the offense. Also, that player cannot be replaced in the game at hand, so his or her team will be short one player. That's a serious disadvantage.

KICKIN' IT FIVE RED CARDS PREVENT A TEAM FROM HAVING ENOUGH PLAYERS TO CONTINUE THE GAME.

CAUTION!

A referee holds up a yellow card, a warning to play fair, if a player commits unsporting behavior, such as arguing with the referees or endangering another player. If a player receives two yellow cards in the same game, he or she is out of the game.

TAKING A DIVE

Sometimes when a player goes in for a tackle, the opposing player will flop to the ground, whine and cry, and pretend to be hurt, hoping to receive a free kick or a penalty kick. This is not sporting behavior, and if caught "taking a dive," a player will be shown a yellow card.

FREE KICKS

A team is awarded a free kick, or is given the ball, if their opponent breaks one of the laws of the game. Common offenses are kicking a player while attempting a tackle or being called for an offside violation. The free kick is taken from the spot of the foul.

EXPLORER'S CORNER

I have never been shown a red card, but yellow cards happen a lot. Once, I fouled a player in the box and gave up a penalty kick. It was a split-second decision as I was trying to stop a goal, so I felt like I was making the right play. The other team did score on the penalty kick, which was tough, having them go up on the scoreboard. But penalties are just part of the game, especially on defense. Good teammates will help you move on after a costly mistake because you'll need to focus on the next play.

PENALTY KICKS

When a defending team commits a foul in the penalty area, the attacking team is awarded a penalty kick. The ball is placed on the penalty spot, and only the goalie can attempt to block the shot. Penalty kicks often result in a goal because they're hard to defend against.

CLUBS AND
LEAGUES

ONE OF THE MANY GREAT
THINGS ABOUT SOCCER IS THAT YOU DON'T
need to be a top pro to play on a team. Soccer clubs exist worldwide, from amateur teams to pro teams. Often, a group of clubs that play at a similar skill level will form a league. Leagues usually have a tournament at the end of a season of play, in which the top team earns a trophy.

AMATEUR CLUBS

Amateur clubs are groups of players who play soccer just for fun, and they are the backbone of soccer leagues around the world. They don't get paid, but there are many more amateur players than pros. Actually, most pros got their start playing with an amateur club. School and recreational teams are also considered amateur clubs. The players don't receive any financial reward and play mostly because they enjoy the game and the competition.

NATIONAL TEAMS

National teams are important to fans, as each country pools its best players together from professional leagues to play in matches such as the FIFA Confederations Cup and the World Cup. The European Championship, played every four years, pits national teams in the Union of European Football Associations against each other.

PROFESSIONAL TEAMS

Professional teams pay players to play, and there are many different levels of pro leagues. As players and teams get better, they may move to a higher level of play. The higher the level, the more money players make. Players often make a living playing for a professional team in a country other than their home country.

City rivals Barcelona and Madrid face off in a Spanish Super Cup match. The Super Cup is the Spanish football championship.

KICKIN' IT CONTINENTAL CHAMPIONSHIPS ARE IMPORTANT SOCCER EVENTS.

A PHOTO GALLERY

GAME DAY

team enters the field of play. All over the world, from parking lot pitches to gleaming modern stadiums, game day is full of excitement. That's because soccer fever is contagious, with billions of fans and players all over the world.

Buddhist monks mingle with the crowd watching a game in Nepal.

Pro soccer players enter the stadium with kids. These kids are called mascots.

U.S. Women's National Team goalkeeper Hope Solo signs fan jerseys at a match.

Some professional soccer stadiums can hold crowds of more than 100,000 people. That's more than the entire population of Appleton, Wisconsin, U.S.A. (73,623)!

The thrill of victory! Players hug their goalkeeper after winning a game.

Japanese fans get into the spirit of the game by wearing soccer ball hats.

Fans dress in their team's colors and wave
flags and scarves at games.

GEAR, GAMES, AND GRANDSTANDS

KITS AND CLEATS

PLAYERS USED TO BE AWARDED A SPECIAL CAP FOR EVERY INTERNATIONAL GAME THEY PLAYED IN.

WHAT CAN AND CAN'T PLAYERS
WEAR ON THE PITCH? YOU GOT IT; THERE'S A LAW.

Law 4 covers equipment. Its focus is on safety. Nobody wants a repeat of the days when broken bones and concussions were just part of the fun. That would not make for a popular sport. Organized soccer is a fast game that can be dangerous to players if the proper equipment isn't worn.

NO BLING

No gold chains or earrings, or jewelry of any kind, can be worn during a soccer match. It could cause an injury if it got tugged on or caught on another player's jersey.

You don't want a cleat coming down hard on your ankle while playing soccer.

KICKIN' IT SOCCER UNIFORMS ARE CALLED KITS, OR STRIPS.

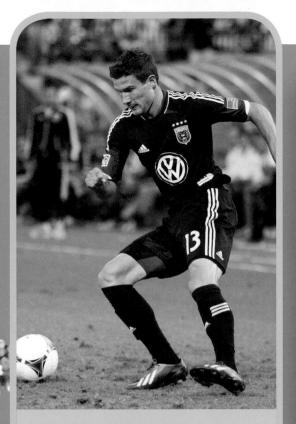

SPONSORS

Sometimes a company sponsors, or supports, a soccer club by helping pay for gear and training equipment. Then that company's name may appear on the front of the club's jerseys.

WHAT GIVES?

Ever notice that there's always one player on a soccer team who's not wearing what everyone else is? It's not a fashion statement. It's just the goalkeeper, and the keeper wears a different uniform than his or her teammates so the referees can tell them apart. The refs need to know who can and can't touch the ball with their hands. Goalkeepers also wear massive cartoonlike gloves with good grip for ballhandling.

JERSEYS usually include a team or club's logo on the front and a player's number and name on the back. Jerseys can be colorful, with national teams often borrowing colors from their country's flag.

SHIN GUARDS are tucked under the socks, and they are a soccer player's best friend. You'll understand why if you ever get kicked or hit in the shin. It hurts. A LOT! And with all the kicking and tackling involved in soccer, players are getting knocked in the shins all the time.

LONG SOCKS are usually the same colors as a player's jersey. Socks protect a player's legs and cover their shin guards.

CLEATS, also called boots, are shoes with spikes, or studs, on the bottom. The longer the spikes, the more traction provided, which helps when playing on a wet pitch. Long spikes also slow you down, so short ones work best on dry days. Cleats keep players from slipping, whether they're dribbling the ball or lining up for a goal shot.

FOOTIE FANATICS

NEARLY EVERY SPORT
BRAGS ABOUT ITS SUPPORTERS.

But soccer fans are a step above all others, not only in their dedication to their team, but in their antics. They scream and yell, sing and chant, sport team colors, and wave flags. Fans line up for days outside a stadium to get tickets to a big game. Supporting their favorite club brings neighbors, villages, cities, and nations together, as people bond over the successes and failures of their favorite teams.

EXPLORER'S CORNER

Soccer fans are the best sports fans in the world. They are fiercely loyal, and love to sing and cheer. It's all part of the culture, and I thank fans for their support every chance I get. For a 2014 World Cup Qualifier between the United States and Costa Rica in Colorado, U.S.A., a crowd of 20,000 fans came to the game. Despite blizzard conditions, they stayed the entire match and never stopped cheering. That's probably one of the craziest things I've ever seen fans do!

IN HIGH GEAR

Want to show your team spirit? Wear your team gear to a game! Soccer scarves were first worn to keep English soccer fans warm while attending games played in cold weather. Now they are symbols of team pride. Every professional soccer team has a team scarf, and fans lift them high during a game. Fans also wear team soccer jerseys to games. Unlike baseball or hockey jerseys, the design of professional league soccer jerseys changes each year. If you're a collector, that's a lot of jerseys to stuff in your closet.

FAN CHANTS

Imagine the deafening sound of 60,000 people in a soccer stadium all singing in unison. Devoted soccer fans not only know their teams, but their team chants as well. Soccer chants are songs or rallying calls sung by the crowd during a game. They are rowdy taunts that make fun of opposing teams and their fans.

WHAT A BLAST!

If you watched any 2010 World Cup games from South Africa, you may remember a constant buzzing noise ringing in your ears. That was the sound made by thousands of plastic horns called *vuvuzelas,* which fans blew into. Vuvuzelas have become a symbol of soccer in South Africa. But several football clubs have banned the noisemakers at games because they are too loud.

CELTIC VS. RANGERS

GREAT RIVALRIES

Nothing brings the crazy out in a fan like playing a rival, the one opponent you hope your team beats more than anyone else. Here are some of the great soccer rivals:

- Boca Juniors and River Plate dominate Argentinian soccer, and after more than 200 meetings, Boca Juniors has the edge, with a 72-66-62 record.

- Barcelona and Real Madrid are not only two of the top teams in Spain, but in all of Europe, having earned (combined) more than 150 titles and tournament trophies.

- Glasgow, Scotland–based teams Celtic and Rangers probably share the longest-standing rivalry, having battled for more than 100 years, during which time they played nearly 400 matches. The rivalry was so entrenched, the two teams were called the Old Firm. The Rangers team no longer plays in the same league as Celtic, though.

SHOW TEAM PRIDE

You yell, you sing, you jump up from your seat! Here are some more wild and wacky ways you can cheer on your team:

- Wear your team's colors, whether it's in a jersey or a scarf, even to a summer game.

- Wave that team flag—especially a flag that represents a national team.

- Channel your inner pop star by singing and chanting your team's songs.

- Paint your face or body using the colors of your favorite team.

SCARF

FACE PAINT

KICKIN' IT THE LOUDEST SOCCER MATCH WAS LOUDER THAN 130 DECIBELS, ENOUGH TO CAUSE EAR DAMAGE.

WORLD CUP

NO OTHER SPORTING EVENT QUITE COMPARES TO THE

World Cup. The tournament as a whole involves nearly every country in the world, thousands of players, and takes years to complete.

EARNING A SPOT

To play in a World Cup match, teams first need to qualify. National teams in each confederation, or qualifying zone, play against each other to earn spots in the World Cup. Because of the number of teams (207 for the 2014 World Cup) wanting to play in the tournament and only a few slots (32) available, there are several qualifying rounds, which take years to complete, as neighboring countries are pitted against each other. Only the best of the best get to play in the World Cup.

KICKIN' IT THE WORLD CUP TROPHY IS MADE FROM 18-KARAT GOLD.

EVERYBODY WATCHES

Not only does the World Cup include more teams and players than any other sporting championship, it is also the most watched event. Fans flock to the host country, sporting their team's colors and cheering them on. Games need to be held in huge stadiums because tens of thousands of fans pack the seats. In the past two World Cups, attendance figures topped three million. There are also billions that tune in on television.

WOMEN'S WORLD CUP

With nearly 30 million female soccer players worldwide, FIFA felt women deserved a tournament equal to that of the men's. So in 1991, the first women's World Cup was played, and tournaments have continued to be played the year following the men's World Cup.

HOME-FIELD ADVANTAGE

Uruguay hosted the first World Cup in 1930, simply because their team won gold in the 1928 Olympics. But since then, FIFA has voted on where the tournament will be held. Hosting the World Cup has its advantages. The host country's national team automatically gets a bid in the tournament. Also, six host countries have won the men's World Cup, while one has won the women's World Cup.

By the Numbers

32 qualifying teams make it to the finals of the World Cup.

19 World Cups have been played since 1930.

8 countries in total have won the World Cup.

6 host countries have won the World Cup.

SUPERSTARS OF SOCCER

SOCCER FANS ALL HAVE THEIR LISTS OF THE GREATEST PLAYERS OF THE GAME. THE SOCCER WORLD IS TEEMING WITH

amazing athletes past and present. Many play or have played for professional clubs all over the world and on the national teams of their home countries in competitions such as the World Cup. Here are just a few of the superstars who have wowed us with their play.

PRESENT STARS

CRISTIANO RONALDO

Professional Team: Real Madrid CF (Spain)
National Team: Portugal
Position: Forward
World Cup Appearances: 2
World Cup Goals: 2
FIFA Player of the Year/FIFA Ballon d'Or: 2008, 2013

Captain of the Portuguese national team, Cristiano's soccer skills have made him one of the highest-paid footballers in the world. He is a fantastic dribbler, and his goal-scoring skills make him a thrill to watch.

CRISTIANO RONALDO

LIONEL MESSI

Professional Team: FC Barcelona (Spain)
National Team: Argentina
Position: Forward
World Cup Appearances: 2
World Cup Goals: 1
Olympic Medals: 1 Gold
FIFA Player of the Year/FIFA Ballon d'Or: 2009, 2010, 2011, 2012

Lionel has not let his small-for-the-game (5' 7" [1.7 m]) frame prevent him from rising to the top of the soccer world.

ROBIN VAN PERSIE

Professional Team: Manchester United FC (Great Britain)
National Team: Netherlands
Position: Forward
World Cup Appearances: 2
World Cup Goals: 2

Robin has a great vision for the game, being able to dissect defenders at a glance and make them pay with his great dribbling and shooting abilities.

Professional teams as of date of publication

KICKIN' IT BRAZIL'S MARTA HAS WON FIFA'S PLAYER OF THE YEAR (WOMEN) FIVE CONSECUTIVE TIMES, 2006–2010.

IKER CASILLAS OF **SPAIN** WON THE **GOLDEN GLOVE AWARD** FOR BEST GOALIE IN THE **2010 WORLD CUP.**

MIA HAMM

Professional Team: Washington Freedom (U.S.)
National Team: United States
Position: Forward
World Cup Appearances: 4
World Cup Championships: 2
World Cup Goals: 8
Olympic Medals: 2 Gold, 1 Silver
FIFA Player of the Year: 2001, 2002

The first female soccer super-star and a pioneer in getting women's soccer recognized, Mia also helped promote women's sports worldwide.

PELÉ

Professional Team: Santos FC (Brazil)
National Team: Brazil
Position: Forward/Midfielder
World Cup Appearances: 4
World Cup Championships: 3
World Cup Goals: 12

Pelé was only 17 when he played in his first World Cup match. His overall speed, footwork, and smarts for the game have led many to consider him to be the best there ever was in the sport.

LEV YASHIN

Professional Team: Dynamo Moscow (Russia)
National Team: Russia
Position: Goalkeeper
World Cup Appearances: 3
Olympic Medals: 1 Gold
Ballon d'Or: 1963

Voted the best goalkeeper of the 20th century, Lev was the first modern-day goalie, darting out of the penalty box to "sweep" the ball out of danger before an attacker could take a shot.

MIA HAMM

SOCCER COMPARISONS

YOU VS. THE PROS

SO YOU WANT TO PLAY SOCCER? FANTASTIC!

Realize that it may take you a while to make it to the pros. But that doesn't mean you can't feel like a pro while playing. Here are some examples of how professional teams and your amateur team may be alike and different.

THE SHIRT OFF YOUR BACK

Your team jersey might include your number on the back. A pro's jersey design changes every year. It shows his or her name and number on the back. The logos of the team's big corporate sponsors are displayed on the front.

THE PITCH

Your soccer pitch is much smaller than a stadium pitch. Yours might also be strewn with dandelions. The pro soccer pitch has teams that maintain the field. Some stadiums even have artificial turf.

THE FANS

Your family probably cheers you on while sitting in lawn chairs or bleachers near the pitch. The fans of professional soccer paint their faces. The crowds cheer loud enough to damage their hearing.

TROPHY WINNERS

Yay! You won! Your trophy is precious, but it's not made from a precious metal like the FIFA Futsal World Cup trophy for indoor soccer. That trophy is made of silver and copper.

KNOCK-YOUR-SOCKS-OFF KICKS

It takes years of training to kick from the inside and outside of your foot. And only the pros can deliver gravity-defying kicks such as the bicycle kick.

Some games don't require much more than a willingness to play. These well-equipped kids in South Africa are learning the rules of soccer by playing it.

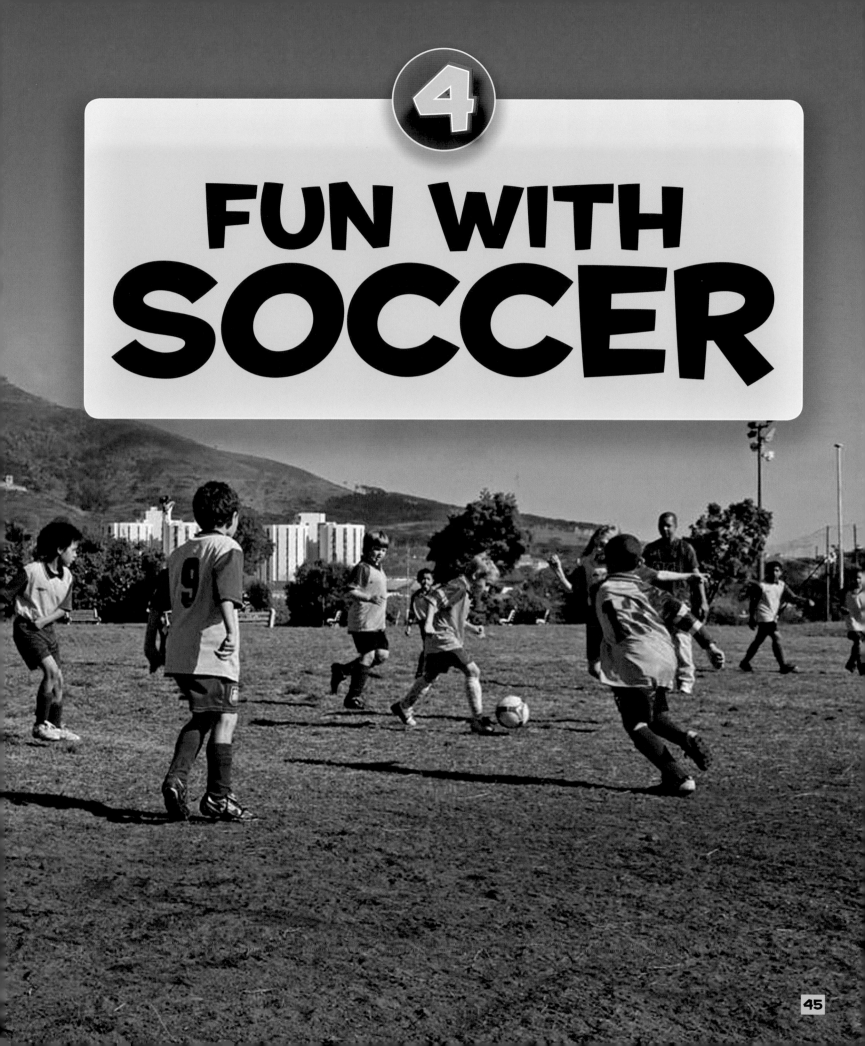

FUN WITH SOCCER

TRAIN LIKE A PRO

ELITE PLAYERS AREN'T
BORN SOCCER STARS. THEY PRACTICE
hard, from a young age, to hone their shooting skills, improve their footwork, and understand the complexities of soccer. Soccer players work hard to keep their bodies in tip-top shape. Match the skill to the exercise to improve your game. Check your training knowledge with the answers at the bottom of the page.

EXPLORER'S CORNER

Young soccer players should be outside practicing as much as possible. And it's just as important to work on the skills you are already comfortable with as it is to work on new ones. That way you keep improving those skills as you get older. As a defender, I find that communication is important. To stop another team from scoring, you need to listen to where the goalie needs you. Passing and dribbling are other basics that every young soccer player should work on.

1 **SKILL: SPEED** (legs) During a game, a sudden burst of speed may be needed to break away or get to a ball before an attacker does.

2 **SKILL: FLEXIBILITY** (legs) Players stop, start, jump, and dive during a soccer game, putting a lot of stress on their legs. Their leg muscles need to be loose to prevent injuries.

3 **SKILL: STRENGTH** (legs) A goalie may need to jump up to block a shot or dive after a ball, so leg strength is crucial.

4 **SKILL: AGILITY** (feet) The ability to quickly change direction and dribble around an opponent is important, especially for attackers.

A. RUNNING SIDE TO SIDE

Running side to side and backward and forward helps to develop quick feet and better balance.

B. RUNNING SPRINTS

Running sprints, or wind sprints, build speed on the pitch. Practice wind sprints on a field by running 50 feet (15 m) ten times. Run on the balls of your feet and lift your knees for more power. Keep your hips tilted forward and your arms at a 90-degree angle. Move your arms in time to your legs with each step.

C. LEG STRETCHES

Stretch your hamstrings, the tendons behind your knees, by bending over at the hips with knees slightly bent and one leg flexed. Hold for ten seconds.

D. LEG LUNGES

Leg lunges build strong legs. Stand with your feet shoulder-width apart, with shoulders back. Step forward with one leg and lower your hips until both knees are bent at a 90-degree angle. Your front knee should be directly above your ankle.

SKILLS SUPPLEMENT

DRIBBLING

One of the most basic soccer skills is dribbling. It's how players move the ball downfield in a controlled manner. Practice dribbling first by kicking the ball and stepping forward with the same foot. Each time you step with that foot, also push the ball forward. Eventually you'll be able to mix it up by using your other foot, and soon you'll be seeing how fast you can run as you dribble. Next, start weaving in and around objects such as trees or cones as you dribble. The key is to keep the ball close to your feet so you can control it.

DRIBBLING

PASSING AND SHOOTING

Precision aim is needed to hit a teammate on a breakaway or to sneak a ball past a goalkeeper. Practice your aim by picking a target and trying to hit it with a ball. To make this exercise more difficult, try hitting the target while dribbling the ball or pick a target that is off the ground—sometimes you'll need to kick the ball over a goalie to score.

NOTE: Kicking with the side of your foot instead of your toes will give you better control.

BALL CONTROL

If you control the ball, you can control the game. But you don't just use your feet to do this. You can head the ball or catch it with your chest (just no hands!). Practice ball control by juggling the ball; first just trying to keep it in the air with your feet, using the tops and sides of your shoes to bounce the ball up in the air. Then start to use your thighs and chest, and lastly your head. By practicing ball control, you'll also learn how soft and hard to kick the ball for touch passes, or passing right away.

CHEST CATCH

KICKIN' IT SOCCER IS SOMETIMES CALLED THE BEAUTIFUL GAME.

SOCCER FARE

SOCCER GAMES ARE A
THRILL, FROM WATCHING THE ANTICS OF
your team's mascot to seeing your favorite player score a goal to enjoying the mouth-watering smell of food wafting in from the concession stands. It takes a lot of energy to shout and sing as you cheer on your team. You need to eat! Along with foods like burgers, hot dogs, pizza, and nachos, some unique foods can be tasted at soccer games.

GLOBAL TASTES

Foods served at stadiums are influenced by the region where a game is played, as well as where the teams and players are from. Many arenas will have food stalls inside, but in some parts of the world, feeding rabid fans is a way for food vendors to earn a living, so they set up stands outside the stadium.

Orange slices are a common halftime snack for recreational league soccer players in North America.

KICKIN' IT SUNFLOWER SEEDS ARE COMMON SNACKS AT SPANISH SOCCER STADIUMS.

POPULAR EATS

FRANKFURTERS

TRADITIONAL FISH & CHIPS

FISH & CHIPS

Chippies are British fish-and-chip shops and trucks that sell pregame eats such as french fries (or "chips") with a curry sauce.

Frankfurters are a staple food at German soccer matches because they are easy to eat without a plate or cutlery.

MEAT PIES & BOVRIL

CAN I TAKE YOUR ORDER?

It's important to keep your strength up while chanting, cheering, and watching a game. Throughout the world, fans in the stands have a number of traditional noshing options. How do your favorite game foods stand up to these offerings?

Meat pies and Bovril, a traditional beef broth, are served at games in England to keep fans warm on cold game days.

PUPUSAS

CABBAGE

These World Cup fans are crazy for ... cabbage?

Pupusas, which are traditional filled tortillas from El Salvador, are served at games in Central America.

MYTH VS. FACT

OKAY, SO AFTER READING

THROUGH THIS BOOK, YOU'RE APPROACHING soccer superstar status. But let's make sure you have the Laws of the Game down. You don't want to be shown a red card. Can you separate the myths from the facts?

A A GAME CAN BE WON WITH A PENALTY KICK.

B IT IS ILLEGAL TO TACKLE A PLAYER FROM BEHIND.

C A BALL JUST NEEDS TO TOUCH THE GOAL LINE TO BE CONSIDERED A GOAL.

D A PLAYER CAN KICK THE BALL OUT OF THE GOALIE'S HANDS.

E PLAYERS OTHER THAN THE GOALIE CAN'T USE THEIR HANDS WHILE THE BALL IS IN PLAY.

A. FACT It doesn't matter how a goal is scored, so if a team gets a penalty kick in the final minutes, it could be a game winner.

KICKIN' IT DURING ONE ARGENTINE CHAMPIONSHIP, 44 PENALTY SHOTS WERE TAKEN IN A SHOOT-OUT.

C. MYTH

While this is true of American football, in soccer, FIFA Law 10 states that the ball needs to be completely across the goal line, and between the goalposts, for a goal to be scored.

D. MYTH

Players can do this, if they want to be shown a yellow card! If a goalie has his or her hands on the ball, the ball is in his or her possession, and no opponents can kick it or interfere with the goalie.

E. FACT FIFA's Law 12 states that a player can't "deliberately handle" the ball, but an accidental touch is okay. The tricky thing here is that it is all up to the referee's judgment, so it's best to play hands-off. The only time players, other than the goalie, are allowed to use their hands is on throw-ins.

B. MYTH While it is difficult to do so, legally there's nothing wrong with tackling this way. For any tackle, as long as it's a clean play that doesn't endanger the opponent, it doesn't matter which direction the tackle came from.

GAME ON!

WHO HELPS TURN UP THE
VOLUME WHEN A TEAM NEEDS SUPPORT?

A team's mascot, that's who. Mascots are like super cheerleaders, only fuzzy and without the pom-poms. Mascots yell, shout, dance, and do acrobatics to get fans riled up and cheering for their team.

MASCOTS ARE ALSO THE NAME FOR **KIDS** WHO **ACCOMPANY PROS** TO THE **PITCH DURING GAMES.**

HAMMERHEAD

LOOKS LIKE TEAM SPIRIT

Teams are commonly named after animals or objects popular to a region or country. Berni the Bear is Bayern Munich's mascot in the German Football Federation League. Hammerhead, a robot with a square head, is the mascot for West Ham United, a team in the English Premier League. A team's mascot may be part of a team's emblem, but more important, some spirited person gets dressed in a hot and stuffy costume to make sure the fans energetically support their team. Mascots are so much a part of the game that many soccer leagues stage mascot battles or games.

Hammerhead is a new mascot—created as the ultimate goal machine and crowd pleaser, in 2011.

FULECO THE ARMADILLO

Not only do teams have mascots supporting them, but large soccer tournaments have mascots to get fans excited. For the 2014 World Cup hosted in Brazil, the mascot is Fuleco, a young armadillo. His name comes from the Portuguese words *futebol* "soccer" and *ecologia* "ecology," so while having a passion for the game of soccer, Fuleco also encourages people to live in an Earth-friendly way.

FULECO

KICKIN' IT RAMMIE THE RAM IS THE DERBY COUNTY FC (ENGLISH FOOTBALL LEAGUE) MASCOT.

MASCOT-O-MATIC

Does your school or league soccer team have a mascot? Have you ever wanted to make one for yourself? What sort of personality would your mascot have? Would it be super cheery, or a strong competitor?

Your mascot should have a cool name too, such as Emmy Eagle, or Reddy Robin. Nutz the Squirrel is the mascot for Scotland's Kilmarnock FC, while Talon the Eagle is the mascot for D.C. United FC.

Think about what your mascot would look like. Draw your mascot. Some mascots look a lot like the animal they portray. Other mascots are simply caricatures or crazy versions of that animal.

While it may be difficult to put together a costume yourself, you and your friends could use face paint to make yourselves look like your mascot.

Or, to cheer on your soccer team, you could simply paint your face like a soccer ball.

It's a mascot dogpile at the annual North American Soccer League mascot soccer game.

Berni the Bear, Bayern Munich's mascot in the German Football Federation League, gets an ear rub from a player.

PHOTO FINISH

BEHIND THE SHOT WITH OMAR GONZALEZ

SOCCER IS THE ULTIMATE

SPORT. JUST ABOUT ANYONE CAN PLAY AND ALL
that is needed to get a game going is a ball. Yet, a soccer game can be a physical chess match when professional players take to the pitch.

Some people criticize soccer for being a low-scoring game—they mistake it for being boring. They don't see the beauty of the sport, or how simple yet challenging it is. Players are constantly moving, passing the ball, and looking for weakness in their opponent's defense. The action may be subtle, but once a chink in the armor is exposed, then ... goal!

It's not easy getting a goal, and as a defender, my opportunities to score are rare. I joined the L.A. Galaxy in 2009, and I have scored and had scoring chances. But the goal pictured here, in an August 2013 game against Italian club Juventus, was an amazing experience. Late in the first half of the match, I collected the ball and passed it to midfield. Then I just kept running upfield. My teammate Juninho passed the ball through the defenders and hit me on the attack. I chipped the ball by goalie Gianluigi Buffon, giving us a 1–0 lead.

That day, we beat Juventus 3–1. It was our first victory over a major European team. You can see from my reaction that it was pure joy. Getting the goal and seeing the crowd going wild was awesome.

The difficulties of scoring turn every ball that hits the net into a moment worth celebrating, for players and fans. That's what makes soccer such a thrill to play and to watch.

L.A. Galaxy defender Omar Gonzalez celebrates after scoring a goal against Juventus during an August 3, 2013, game at Dodger Stadium in Los Angeles, California, U.S.A.

AFTERWORD

THE BEAUTIFUL GAME

KICKING A BALL AROUND IS ALMOST INSTINCTIVE, SOMETHING WE NATURALLY DO AS CHILDREN,

and something even adults enjoy doing. Maybe that's the reason ball games have been played throughout history. Soccer merely takes that love of knocking a ball across the yard and watching it bounce away and turns it into a game. A game that in one sense is fun to play among neighborhood friends because of its simplicity, yet is also a game that can be watched and admired as professional players show off their amazing athletic abilities.

Why is soccer so popular? Probably because it is the ultimate sport, in that you need very little to play it. No expensive equipment, just a ball and a little room to kick it around. But that one piece of equipment can lead to a complex and challenging game with professional players dueling it out with their dribbling and kicking skills. Not only that, but nearly everyone can play soccer, young and old. You don't need to be a pro, as amateur leagues, schools, and recreational centers organize games just about everywhere and for just about everyone.

Soccer is also a game that reaches beyond people's differences. Just drop a ball in the middle of two groups of players that don't speak the same language or have the same religion, and a soccer game will bind them in play.

SCORING BIG WITH YOUTH PROGRAMS

Soccer fans show support for their favorite team by chanting and screaming and painting their faces. In return, professional soccer gives back to the community by spreading the joy of the game. Some teams sponsor youth teams so that kids have the opportunity to play soccer. Other teams hold camps to give budding soccer stars the chance to hone their skills while being encouraged by professional players.

Major League Soccer, the top professional soccer league in the U.S. and Canada, sponsors the Active Bodies Active Minds program. The program helps kids stay active on the field and in the classroom and promotes living healthy every day.

Kids show off their skills at a United Soccer Club tournament. The program is run by United for D.C., a nonprofit group organized by D.C. United.

The Women's World Cup is the most important international women's soccer event. The 2015 event will be held in Canada.